Imagine That

The one book written
just for you
no matter who you are!

THINK WHAT YOU WOULD ACCOMPLISH IF
YOU ONLY KNEW HOW. THE AUTHOR REVEALS
YOUR NATURAL ABILITY TO DO ANYTHING
YOU SINCERELY WANT TO DO WITH DRAMATIC
FLAIR AND PERFECTION.

Author: Robert Edgar
Publisher: Robert Seay
PO Box 96093, Las Vegas, NV 89193

ISBN 978-1-734-3633-1-9

Introduction

This book is for everyone who questions the mystery of human existence, the power of the subconscious, or believes all things are possible, if you are determined to succeed.

This book has been developed with everyone in mind, the entertainer, the trucker, the executive, the politician, the sports figure, the waitress, the scientist, the family - it's written for all religions and faiths.

It's for students. It's for all races and all ages.

Before you read any further though, I want you to take note of your surroundings.

Everything you see was brought into existence through someone's imagination, including this book, and this book is going to guide you to an understanding you may have never considered.

Know this, we are all destined to live a reality of our own making, good or bad. There is no escaping, because it is fixed by universal law.

Life requires action from you and me to do something with our lives. To be creative and to be responsible.

Grade school tried to do that for us, middle school, high school, college, marriage and the military, too.

So, we really have no excuse if we have failed at anything or at any stage of our lives, and no, we can't say we weren't warned.

The most important responsibilities we have are supporting our family's basic needs, health, welfare, and education.

No matter what your age, if what you've been doing hasn't worked out the way you wanted, then you have no choice but to listen to the voice of reality if you want to be successful.

Take just a moment to realize that you are not trapped in a helpless situation but instead, have been presented with an enormous opportunity.

If your life and what it represents is unsatisfactory, then you must ask yourself, if not you, then who has the answers that can turn your failures into winners and move the pieces around to where you can at least see through the confusion. You're a smart person, or you would have already stopped reading this book. But don't worry, no one is trying to get you to join a cult or become a member of a new religion.

I want you to simply consider for a moment that someone is going to give you something without any strings attached. Free! Absolutely free!

Only once in a lifetime does something so revolutionary present itself to us in this way.

There is no cost or obligation attached.
It's a gift like you have never known, and for the uninformed masses, it means escape - total freedom from everything that has kept them imprisoned emotionally or kept them from enjoying even the bare necessities of life.

So, take advantage of this gift, and realize for once in your life, today, you are the luckiest person on this planet.

You can stop worrying right now about money, health concerns or any other obstacle keeping you from advancing to your rightful place in life.

I want you to realize first who you are, and then ask yourself this question…Why haven't you taken the time to get to know yourself better?

This isn't such a strange question. Most people truly do not know who they are and what powers they possess, because they have always sought answers to these important questions from others instead of investigating themselves.

Do you think others know you better than yourself?

Well, some might, on the outside, but not on the inside.

Forget other people, psychologists, psychiatrists, psychotherapists, friends, etc. Stop!

The inscription over the ancient Greek temple in Delphi reads, "Know thyself."

Socrates said, "To know thyself is the beginning of wisdom."

After all, what does it hurt to be wise and act accordingly?   Isn't that why we seek higher education?

What I'm proposing is this.

Simply give yourself a chance for once because until you know yourself, you know nothing!

Get to know yourself, and step away from the herd.

Sure you'll be exposed but you were made to stand out in life and that doesn't mean you have to fit into the same slot as everyone else.

Dead fish are the only things that go with the flow!

Don't look at your life as something negative.

That's the trap that has most people imprisoned and non-productive. They simply aren't living, and worse yet, they don't even know it!

You will either continue serving the dictates of others, or you will take your life back and start putting it to good use. And I'll tell you how to do just that.

You will make this reality serve you by taking charge of your life first and then controlling every aspect of it going forward.

When you recognize the power of self and what that really means, you are free.

It all boils down in part to recognizing your ability to think and act on a deeper level without restriction.

The next step is action, without it you will remain stalled and suspended in fantasy.

"The journey to a thousand miles begins with the first step" is found in Chapter 64 of the Tao Te Ching, 604 BC by Laozi.

Also accredited to Confucius of the same period.

You only have one life - one - so live it freely powerfully and abundantly. Now, let's get busy creating you a new mindset and a new and clear beginning.

The book you're holding is worth a thousand times what you paid for it because this book will set you up for life.

Don't loan it or allow it to be copied. Never let it leave your possession.

However, make sure you alert at least ten of your closest and most trusted friends of its existence and then have them tell everyone they know and everyone they know and so on.

Safeguard it with the same protection as you would with your fortune, because it is that and much, much, more.

II

III

Acknowledgements

Praises to the armies of researchers and writers including those introspective confidence building philosophers and truth seekers who pass along so freely, new discoveries that benefit and enlighten the masses.

Out of nothing, dreams are realized when a thought connects with the action of a motivated and determined person.

The discoveries made and realized through the imagination of determined believers is proof that we really do have no limitation.
Every thought you have is real and for a reason.
Every thought you have means something.

Take time to listen to the quietness of your soul, and say to your imagination out loud if necessary, I'm listening.

Always welcome knowledge and wisdom by clearing your mind and listening to your thoughts, for they are speaking directly to you.

Learn to understand the difference between useless mental chatter and meaningful, useful thought.

Some of the most valuable discoveries you will ever make will not be found in books or classrooms, but by listening to your thoughts and conversing with your spirit and imagination.

Disclaimer

This disclaimer is to state clearly the intention of the author and the publisher.

The information contained within is not intended to diagnose, prescribe or replace any doctor or medical practitioner's instruction. Nor is it intended for diagnosis of disease(s) including, diagnosis of an individual's mental health issues, but suggested that all individuals seek instruction from professionals in their specialized medical or psychological fields.

This book contains no legal advice or dispensation of information in any form that might mislead or confuse an individual's understanding of the metaphysical, incorporeal, or supernatural.

Part One

1

Introduction

Hello, I'm Robert.

Thank you for purchasing this book. Whether you're someone just starting to realize the magnificent powers you already possess through your imagination, or you're someone well advanced and aware that there are no limitations other than those we place upon ourselves…the reality is,

there is nothing impossible.

What I have come to understand and what you are about to experience in this collection of information is that life is really an ever evolving mystery that we must pay very close attention to or we'll be missing out on untold fortunes.

Most of us never think that we're hearing information of any substance anymore because the deep thinking philosophers are deceased and we are suspicious of most of our modern philosophers.

We have forgotten that you should know the tree by the fruit it bears.

Simply speaking, life's hard to understand for most because, as it seems to me, we're consistently looking in the wrong place for answers to even life's simplest questions.

We now know through scientific study that the answers to all of life's questions already exist and always have.

What questions then or actions do we take that will cause a surrendering of these hidden treasures to become clear to us? Where are the answers we think we're in need of to even come close to understanding this foggy mystery?

On the surface and in the beginning of our lives, research is now beginning to show that our experiences are nothing more than warm up exercises and practice runs at what real life is most definitely going to surprise us with.

So, before we venture further, remember, there is a key to getting the jump on living a quality life.

First, let's understand since childhood our minds have been filled with what everyone else thought was best for us, how we should live our lives, what career would be best suitable, what kind of person to marry, where to live, and what kind of career to pursue.

Well, as you can see, that was bad advice because we as children had no knowledge or real experience of other places, careers, or anything self-fulfilling and now, all we have is regret for not having dealt with anger, frustration, disappointment, deprivation, deception, and failure head on.

We thought, 'a career like that' is obviously meant for someone else. Mom would never approve. Dad would be very disappointed. What would all my friends think?

Looking back, we allowed everyone else to live our lives, and we never even came close to knowing who we are! Sad to say but here we are. We have one thing going for us, however, it's never too late to take control and live life on our terms.

Take action, wake up your imagination, realize this, you have one life, and it would be a shame and disaster to waste it by living other people's unsatisfied and unfulfilled dreams.

Just like old clothes you'll never wear again, old toys you're never going to play with again, or anything else you've outgrown, it's a waste of time and something you must ultimately let go of.

You've been condemned to living life in a prison cell of self incarceration by your refusal to accept the gifts that are rightfully yours. But today you are pardoned and free to soar to heights only dreamed of, or go places you have always wanted and to realize it doesn't matter your age, your financial status, your race. You can dream as large as you can imagine, and this life of frustration and anxiety, along with those toys or clothes or trinkets, are destined to the trash bin never to restrict you ever again.

Take all your negativity, your bad experiences, and embrace new challenges with excitement. Start crowding out and replacing all the negativity with unrelenting optimism.

You must begin the process of being born again and at this point admit that you know absolutely nothing and are willing to accept only the truth as was originally intended for you.

It doesn't matter if you're in a penthouse or panhandling on the street, you have no choice but to start from where you are, because there is no such thing as waiting for the right time.

You must realize everything begins with the first step, and of course, you must keep nudging your spirit, get its attention, pay close attention to your thoughts going forward.

At times, you, like everyone else will run into frustration and uneasiness during your transition. But know this and remember, all that confuses you is temporary. The sunshine always returns after the rain. It's those dark times that makes you appreciate the light.

What I originally and early on discovered about myself in this mysterious life turned out to be my own naive wish that friends and associates would be nice enough to approve of the direction I was taking in my career and would remain sincere with their good luck wishes, and the always readily available, "Let me know if I can help."

I quickly discovered that success of everything, no matter what, even the most basic idea or plan is based entirely on the strength of its foundation.

For me this gave way to critical self analysis.

I found like so many others, that I was searching outwardly for answers that inwardly already existed.

I assumed, respectfully, that others were more attuned and privileged to the kind of information I was seeking and obviously needed in order to understand what I was dealing with, and, because of age difference, advanced experience, and possibly their specialized education, they would never entertain even the remotest possibility of tutoring me.

So, I retired that thought and got busy digging deeper into critically specialized information, mysticism and relative studies, etc.

I found there were those who believed in parallel universes and were able at will to visit these universes through imagination, manipulation, and/or deep meditation.

I read the bible and determined through religious teachings and philosophies that God, as many refer to, is one form of extreme intelligence, and that our subconscious living within travels with us wherever we go, therefore proving we are never alone.

Still, I felt left out of being in control of even a small portion of my life, and that was uncomfortable.

Having another's control psychologically, philosophically, or religiously just didn't fit well into my own plans.

Surprisingly, I had no guilt but felt somewhat empowered instead when I decided to take upon myself all control, sever the philosophic and manmade religious tethers and go it on my own.

After I decided to take full control of my spiritual and creative, as well as personal life, I knew I had taken on an awesome responsibility.

I discovered that there existed within me, unlimited possibility, and if I tapped into this discovery properly by focusing my attention with undiluted intensity I could command life to not only serve me but empower me as well.

I discovered that answers to all of our questions already exists somewhere and are simply waiting to be discovered and put to use.

I discovered that answers to everything are everywhere, in all things, all around us. And you know something, I for some reason early on in my youth just happened to inherently already believe, know, feel, and accept this grand design at face value, and without question or reservation.

The houses we live in, the cars we drive, the clothes we wear, even the utensils we use to eat with, and yes, the medicines designed to help keep us healthy or cure us from disease was at one time just a thought or an idea in someone's imagination.

An idea, a manifestation, corporeal, something of nonphysical existence transformed into a physically tangible entity. How is that possible?

Giving notice and attention to the invisible and massaging it into form by working with and putting one's thoughts on paper, it then becomes the first step of an existing physical reality.

Look around you, the evidence is everywhere. It's in your office, your home, the restaurants you visit, everywhere.

There's no more electricity today than there has ever been. It's always been there, all the time, waiting to be discovered by someone who understood and believed it existed and believed that it was worth bringing into physical form and under managed control instead to benefit humanity at large.

Do you think there's more wind, sun, daylight or darkness today than there has ever been? The answer is absolutely NO!

There are going to be discoveries that some will make in association with all those elements that will undoubtedly benefit us all - something directly associated with the wind, daylight, darkness, sun, etc.

There will be discoveries that will broaden the human pathway and bring about needed results, eventually capturing and controlling what has never physically existed before as we know it.

It's like the beginning of a casual or nonspecific conversational exchange among random participants where no one understands for sure the direction the conversation is taking when it first starts, but more than likely ends up a pleasant outcome and positive experience for everyone as creative minds and imaginations work together bringing about the best in everyone.

There is an eastern philosophy that says, "When the student is ready, the teacher will appear."

I'm sure you've heard that phrase, but is it really true?

You just seem to know when you're ready for the right thing to happen and accept it as already a reality.

Against all odds and opinions, you discover your imagined reality is all that matters.

The same with, "seek and you will find" or "knock and it will be opened unto you." Dig in, in other words, take action and know you're right, and simply keep forging ahead.

Use every means available to discover the truth.

Never succumb to laziness, and never leave anything unanswered, no matter how small.

Life requires action! Listen, the landscape of this world is scattered with failed attempts and evidence of lost courage.

Research everything, both large and small, but above all, seek the truth.

Unrealized and scattered dreams of those who quit or failed to follow through are everywhere.

Numerous times lives have been lost by those who gave up and drowned only inches from the shore, or died in fires only inches from the doorway.

Don't let confusion or temporary loss of imagination and direction get in your way. Don't let friends or family discourage you.

You will be better off if you never discuss your plans, dreams, or ideas with anyone who is not part or partner with you.

Within you and you alone lives the power and spirit to go one more day, one more mile, one more step.

The only one who can defeat you, is you. Make that clear before you ever undertake anything.

There's a partial verse in a song that I wrote that says, "It's a long climb from the bottom to standing here in my tracks, but once you know where you want to go, ain't nobody but you holding you back."

Weld that verse in your mind and realize this - only you authorize failure or success in your life, only you.

I don't care what or who comes against you, you alone authorize acceptance or rejection.

Remember this, within you lives many a dream waiting to be realized. And know this also, your consistent internal focus will create that external or outer physical reality when you are ready to accept it.

Within your amazing imagination lies the answer to all you will ever need to know.

You have access to all mysteries existing within you, and the ability to achieve your goals no matter how extravagant they may seem.

I don't remember who said, "When you love something more than you're afraid of it, you can achieve anything."

Life will never serve you properly if you are determined to fail, because quitting is easy, and anyone can do that.

Never take the avenue of least resistance unless it's the proper thing to do for the greater good of all involved.

However, in every phase of your life you will find that action is the first thing required following a worthwhile thought.

You must know within that statement the end is determined by the many steps involved to accomplish each intricate function of what the dream was or has become before you can realize the physical functioning of what was once just a thought.

In all reality your mind conceives an idea and grows that idea by and of itself, the same as a developing child in the mother's womb.

Your mind is impregnated with thought, and unless you nourish that thought with continued imagination and encouraging attention, that thought will become nothing more than a mental miscarriage.

That thought will fail to develop into any physical, psychological or useful reality but will remain stalled and abandoned in the back rooms of your mind.

Why?

Because energy never dies. It either remains dormant and serves no one, or possibly by mental telepathy, escapes toward the urgent calling and need of another's more aggressive thought in progress or by possibly someone's more passionate dream in need of such an idea.

Can you ever return to such a thought?

The answer to that is always yes, but only as long as the mind or body is physically alive will that thought be unique to that person.

This is not to say that someone else has not had the same thought.

There are thoughts flying around that were never acted on and are free for the taking by anyone with a more aggressive imagination.

You must have, at one time or another, encountered people whom have said with great surprise to you I'm sure, "Oh, I had that very same thought."

This is proof enough that thoughts are real and have an existence, and whomever is willing to adopt or use them for a greater good, other than just allowing them to vegetate, is welcome to them.

It is my firm belief that we all have a command over the invisible, and can at will, call into existence powerful angels of deliverance from harm, failure, or loss, and with concentrated determination, control our own unique inner space where all things exist and all things through the use of our imagination are available to us, if we truly desire the experience.

The bible states clearly that we can be granted or given the desires of the heart.

What are the desires of your heart that lead to and give way to the inevitable question, how big can you dream?

Inner space is just as big as outer space, if that even matters. But still, there is no limit to either because of our unique and unlimited gift of imagination.

Inner space can never be smaller than outer space, or less important because of true balance.

Consider your imagination likened to that of the Hubble telescope, always probing and searching for the new, the undiscovered, the unknown, why?

Let me tell you.

Everything in existence is first born of imagination.

All of outer space is born of inner space first, through imagination.

Everything in existence physically was at one time non physical and only thought.

Our imagination requires energy, and through the combination of imagination and energy ,we transform thought into physical existence. Just look around you.

Given the fact that we, the human race, are born to die tells me that we are also born to live.

We have a window of opportunity between life and death in which we can create spectacular realities and develop amazing and realistic opportunities for future generations from trillions and gazillions of thoughts alone.

Multiply that by the billions of people all possessing and processing these invisible thought patterns.

You are not here to drift from dream to dream like a particle of dust without intelligence.

You my friend, are born with the ability and opportunity for greatness. And, if you will act on just one thought that feels important to you, you will see gigantic and genius sized accomplishment arise out of nothing.

Until I decided to write this book, it didn't exist. But when I wrote the first word, I gave it life.

First, a thought, then a decision, putting it on paper, taking action, staying with it until it takes physical form, shape and has meaning.

There is a process in our lives we will follow whether we like it or not. Unless we determine ourselves to break away from the herd and dig our way out of the wasteful common mindset of nonproductive nothingness, we are no more useful or unique than that particle of dust. Therefore, we are subject to a natural environmental and evolutionary process of being tossed, kicked, shoved and slammed by some invisible process which will naturally and over time take charge and determine our existence for us, if we continue doing nothing.

We then in our weakened and helpless state are overcome by the elements and recycled back into the environment where the rain, sun, wind, etc., once critical to our survival, now become instruments of our demise. Because of the inevitable and continuous exposure to the above, we now, in our weakened and diminished state, will ultimately meet with definite extinction and start to physically disassemble.

It's the same as any structure left unattended.

Oceans are, and always have been, critical in the supply chain of unique edible life-saving properties.

Consider the human food supply chain and know at the same time pollution and dead lifeforms are food for scavengers at the ocean bottom.

Nature doesn't need encouraging, it just works.

In tying all of this together we come to the understanding and conclude that nature's grand design is not an accident, and nothing nor anyone will stop the expression or expansion of nature, or for that matter, change its course.

This is all very evident even as you watch a plant grow. Bamboo can reach up to 3 feet of growth in one 24-hour period, simply by its unique nature.

In the desert where no visible signs or evidence of life seem to exist, it will spring to life, bringing with it a variety of flowers or plants that cover an entire landscape after an overnight shower.

You see, sometimes attention, cultivation, and a little nurturing is all it takes to see the other side of a reality that most certainly exists but is hidden just outside of our conscious, psychological, or visual reach.

A reality we fail to notice because we have allowed our senses to become diminished, and therefore, leave us unexcited and inattentive.

We all possess the propensity to deceive ourselves, even though most times it's unintentional.

But now, more attentive to our senses, we begin to awaken to an altogether new and different world that has been hidden, just ever so slightly, out of our sight or our reach.

As we evolve from what was once an unaware reality and discover this awesome and unique world of possibilities that before never existed in our limited state of blurred and stunted consciousness, now is broken through and is vividly alive.

Every possibility in existence will speak to us, if we're willing to listen.

Right now, somewhere in this world the darkness of uncertainty in someone's mind is being shattered and a shimmering new awareness of human spirit and potential has seen its first sunrise.

We haven't been totally unaware of our surroundings overall, we just haven't been totally awake to them, and that in part is what makes it possible to merge with this new found awareness with ease and excitement as our senses awaken like a new and budding flower at dawn's first light.

We are discovering for the first time this powerful awareness that has been living within but never awakened or realized.

As a member of the human family, some of us have had this innate awareness ever since childhood of something much larger and greater than ourselves.

Born with an acute awareness that alerts us when we are doing something unnatural or immoral such as stealing, cheating, or lying.

We develop guilty feelings, and those guilty feeling are telling us to wake up and return to our natural selves because we have made a mistake.

If we catch ourselves in time by coming to our senses and return to the proper and natural course of direction we were on before, we'll naturally and automatically reverse directions and heal what we have harmed.

Mostly ourselves!
Confessing to the wrong and asking for forgiveness from the person we might have harmed or offended makes us feel better because we have

freed our conscience of the heavy weight of shame that hangs around our necks like an invisible medallion for everyone to see, unconsciously of course.

When you are guilty of such, there is an uncomfortable awareness in those that encounter you and a keen sense that something is very wrong just being in your presence.

We also will no longer carry the burden of guilt around with us which only served to distract and hinder our state of awareness and slow our psychological growth.

When we realize that we have ultimately only hurt ourselves by wronging another, it is signal enough to make us realize we are guided by an always watchful consciousness and that this consciousness is in all reality, attempting to protect us from ourselves.

Like magic somehow, we are all very capable of getting back on track naturally if we'll be open to simply applying some sincere apologetic regret to the wound.

That unintended spur of the moment action when we harm another is like being lost in the fog, disoriented and unsure of what to do next. But it also enables us to find a way back to our naturally solid footing and regain the richness of a balanced and redemptive equilibrium.

Another great thing we possess is the ability to redeem ourselves by the forgiveness we extend to others for their misguided action against us and the dimming of their vision.

We have, living within each of us, the power and ability to forgive others.

Never do we have to get approval from the morals board of some self-appointed self-righteous hierarchy.

We alone as individuals possess the power to forgive and the authority to dispense that forgiveness at will and in abundance.

We have also discovery powers and understanding that real power is the power of self control.

I have faith in the fact that we are multi-functional beings for a reason and are not just on this earth to live, work, and die but to co-create, learn, and educate others who may not yet be aware of these priceless gifts that are in abundance and free for the taking.

If we would treat life like a giant Easter egg hunt, none of us would ever be disappointed, because searching and finding our reward or our life's treasure is somehow a built-in guarantee.

That being said, we now know the treasures of life are hidden within us for the purpose of self-discovery and enlightenment.

Putting them to use for all to benefit from is part of the mystery of life.

We are to take what has been given or supplied us and give it new meaning in the name of usefulness through co-creation.

We have the natural ability to command great wealth, perfect health, and happiness by determining to do so and by using whatever we have to make it so. "Action is key and required here."

Making up our mind to accomplish something and acting on it will create it through whatever frame of mind we may choose, positive or negative.

The reality is created when you mix portions of passion, determination, faith, and action in equally blended and compatible parts.

Our minds and our imagination create. We, therefore, become what we dwell on or affix our attention to.

It is impossible to be stopped from accomplishing what we set our minds to, as long as we continue moving in the direction of our goal.

That thought alone tells me clearly that nothing can stop us because nothing exists that is impossible. Nothing!

If you don't yet know how to positively awaken your spirit, you will by the time you finish this book, because what I have written, anyone can understand.

This book's main purpose is designed to make it impossible for you to live an unfulfilled existence unless you are just determined to do so.

Accept the fact that you are blessed, you as an individual, you are someone of great worth regardless of appearance, race, status, ability or disability.

The majority will fail in life because they will never discover unstoppable drive, faith, and that burning passion present and living within.

This is brought on because they have accepted life as being only an existence for a time.

Let's start from before the beginning of your physical life, while in the womb. Understand that your spirit was the one with the motivation and energy to race ahead of all that existed.

You were the one who desired to be born. You fought to survive in the womb and grew into who you are presently. Need I say more? You are here because you wanted to be, you owe and are responsible to and for yourself.

You have completed half of your journey already just by being here, and I am here to help you continue through to completion, should you stumble.

You are just now beginning to awaken to an even more exciting revelation in life, and this is not the time to stop or slow down.

Your awareness is evolving and expressing itself in full bloom, more elevated, more advanced, a more powerful reality than you've ever imagined awaits.

Therefore, to stop or reverse your course at this point would be disastrous. But to continue is elevation, new awareness, new discovery, leading to and advancing toward greater personal enlightenment.

Again, this is all about you.
I understand if you're tired or disappointed but this is not the time to slow down.

Wake your spirit and move forward because unknown by you still is that your reward is waiting just ahead.

Accept it and receive it, for it is a beautifully adorned, indescribable, unique and rich, one of a kind treasure, "The likes of which has never before existed in your life."

Remember early on in the first few pages I told you about people who had drowned only inches from the shore?

Well, I don't want anyone's life becoming such a statistic if I can help it. Stay awake and stay with me, and we'll both reach the finish line in first place.

The first part of your life was spent in preparation so you could and would understand and appreciate the fullness and reward of the rest of it.

I want you to lean forward, lean into the expectations of great things coming to you, starting now.

No matter how old or how young you are or the condition of your health, learn and do unique and different things to generate confidence and stamina, and do it everyday.

Find a purpose for living one more day, because your faith will make it so, your faith will make you whole.

I want you to become excited about your life. Your unlimited future and potential starts now.

I know what it means to have dreams or aspirations and not have a clue as to how to make them happen.

I know also what it means to feel lost in a world that seems to have no idea of your value, your talents, or even care to understand your existence.

We all have within us a desire to be recognized for our talent as well as our expressions and opinions and also, our value as an individual.

Your opinion of yourself is your reality - good or bad. A lot of time the majority will get opinion and fact confused, especially when someone is charismatic or has what seems is the voice and appearance of authority.

The political arena is one common area which has in fact produced numerous failures and disappointments over and over, never learning the simplest lessons of what not to do. It continues to destroy, slander, and divide instead of reversing failure and moving upward and into a productive and positive direction of success that benefits everyone, which is its sole responsibility, after all.

Political greed, unregulated, uncontrolled power has also cost numerous societies great wealth and untold millions upon millions of innocent lives. There is going to be a price to pay for this!

Political impropriety will continue standing as a living testament of shame etched in the annals of our nation's history as a living reflection of unforgivable mistakes and more importantly, as a reminder to the leaders of tomorrow that impeccable character and integrity in all things does matter and above all is a must, because we the people will demand it!

Part Two

2

The future is yours, regardless of your past, and if you'll use your talent wisely, I'll prove it.

Honor my humble request and continue with me, because the best is yet to come for all of us, and I promise you that.

Learn to accept and understand who you are. This is hard for most, and most don't know who they truly are, because they have only learned to be what they have been taught by their caregivers or authority figurers.

Identify and take pride in the fact that you, as a single individual, a living breathing being, uniquely represent the highest level of intelligence ever known to exist in the history of mankind.

Consider this....

Why would an intelligent person, desperately wanting to live, refuse oxygen or a blood transfusion? That's profoundly stupid some would say, and others would call it insane. Yet it's what we do, knowing the truth, we refuse to believe it and remain instead, feeling guilty grappling in the dark searching for the light that we continue to destroy. We had rather struggle endlessly proving nothing than accept what we know the truth to be.

If you are reading or listening to this book for the first time, I want you to remember a time when you were convinced you couldn't go another day or take another step, but miraculously you did, and eventually the pain, disappointment, and heartbreak subsided.

Those painful experiences through time somehow have slowly faded, and you now find it hard to remember the actual pain or emotion attached.

The disappointment and anguish of those moments have disappeared, but your subconscious has not forgotten and never will. That is what you draw your strength from going forward.

Taking that first step forward, then another, and another. Those steps will energize you, and new meaning and success will follow.

It will every time.

If you'll understand that the power to do anything you choose is in you, living and supporting your imagination, waiting patiently for a signal from you to continue.

Time is significant and perpetual, and you are in for the ride of your life, if you'll stay expectant.

You can make all of life's experience conform to your wishes unless you are traumatized and incapable of choosing. Otherwise, you have no excuse but to go for it and get all you can out of the experience of being alive.

Memories, remember, good or bad, fade but time never fades or fails. It continues marching on.

We live and die. But I believe we have a purpose, and that is to be the best we can be, given the time we have.

We can make life better for all and bring innovation, enlightenment, and discovery to everyone. That sets us apart from other life forms in the sense that we as the human species are unique in wanting to leave a legacy that will benefit those we leave behind.

You've heard the phrase, it's better to give than receive, why?

It's very simple why.

Life never fails to consistently reward the giver both financially and in recognition.

Consider Thomas Edison, Henry Ford, Bill Gates, Alexander Graham Bell, Steve Jobs, Jeff Bezos, including those whose medical breakthroughs have saved countless lives. There are thousands of other inventors, scientists and billionaire corporate geniuses that have enriched our world with such amazing success and discoveries.

It would be naive to think they weren't abundantly blessed in the process.

Your contribution is no less important even if it's only lending a hand or investing some time in a neighborhood project, or helping someone recover from a small disaster.

Be glad you have the opportunity to help someone in need, because this is a blessing in and of itself.

Your imagination is your future, and you'll discover that investing quality time in yourself is critical to your success.

Your true self naturally knows and refuses to be deceived but rather guides you carefully toward your goals.

Listen to your thoughts because they are attempting to guide you.

Know what the repercussions would be as a result if you take your eyes off the prize or became distracted negatively.

The ego would jump at the chance to explain because it lives only for self and will waste no time on stealing the spotlight to satisfy its own gluttonous recognition, be it good or bad.

When you are true to yourself, you will walk in the light and therefore never have need of another's approval or opinion, ever!

This thought alone is a quantum leap for many but also provides an escape from what may very well could be years of confusion and failure.

Once you experience the light that sets you free, the truth and the possibility of what is gained by it will have you thinking twice before you ever mislead anyone ever again, yourself included.

I don't care what the end game or profit gain in your favor may appear to be.

The most successful, respected, likable, well-rounded people of all walks of life are those who know and own themselves.

They know who they are and have no need of other's opinions directing their steps, because they are already walking in the light, and everyone who meets them somehow knows it also.

Remember this, you can do anything you really want to do no matter how impossible it may seem. But when you do it with integrity you have found the key to real and lasting success.

When you really want to do something you'll find a way to accomplish the goal.

When you don't want to, you will find an excuse not to.

It's an involuntary reaction, and you can't help but perform it when asked.

These are simple identifying markers and will save you lots of time in clearing the way if you are paying attention.   But let's return to the main focus of this book and that is to exercise the power of your imagination until it responds to you like a weight lifter's muscles when needed.

I want to stop here and deliver to you what you may have never heard before, and it's most important you know this before we continue on.

STEPS IN CREATING REALITY

There are mechanics involved in the way you direct your mind when attempting to achieve your goals.

It is so simple that even the brightest minds never mention it. And for some reason unbeknownst to me, they skip right over it, taking for granted that you must already know and that is simply this. The two most important steps in achieving anything is having a clear understanding that your conscious mind is your imaginative mind, and your subconscious mind only follows orders.

In other words, your imagination.
Your subconscious mind is the architect that takes action, follows the orders of your conscious mind, develops the plan, and brings it all together for your benefit.

This is beyond human understanding, and for whatever reason, there is reluctance in many to accept this as a reality.

Your subconscious mind does not evaluate what the conscious mind wants. It simply responds to the conscious mind's request.

Your creative, imaginative or conscious mind conceives an idea and hands it over to the ever reliable subconscious mind.

Now understand this, once this action takes place between the two minds, the subconscious mind is instantly responsive to any and every suggestion your conscious or creative mind feeds it.

It's ready and willing to act and does so without hesitation when impressed.

It acts as instructed or purposed by the conscious mind. Functioning without question because that is its entire nature.

It does not hesitate or evaluate anything in terms of value or worth but acts on the orders of the imaginative, conscious, or creative mind.

It has no opinion, and it does not evaluate whether any command is moral or immoral.

Its nature is to deliver to your creative mind all its wishes, regardless of size or value.

There is nothing too big or too small for the subconscious to achieve.

That puts you in position of unlimited possibility.

Get to know and believe this intimately.

There is no difference in size, importance or value to the subconscious. The subconscious mind is blind to everything but what its responsibilities are.

Instead, everything is the same in value or importance to your subconscious mind.

This will help you understand the rest of this book from here on out if it becomes confusing in the latter pages.

I want you to write yourself a mantra of confidence so strong that you are able to speak to the invisible and expect a response without concern, doubt, or worry - the same as Jesus did when he commanded Lazarus, a dead man of four days, to come forth from the tomb when he said, "Father, thank you, that you have heard me, with confidence and expectancy." Then he called Lazarus forth and Lazarus rose and walked out of the tomb.

I believe the above statement is symbolic and carries such weight and speaks such truth that we are capable of performing the very same power of expression to our own satisfaction.

Things and powers not human will happen as your faith begins lining up with the dynamic of your mantra.

In the book of James in the bible you can find this verse which clears it all up if you're really paying attention.

Faith without works is dead. Need I say more? You must act on faith, believing it is done.

You, my friend, have only to believe to achieve. By taking action you are putting your faith to work, end of story.

This is confusing to some, but to most it's simple. If you fail to act, faith believing nothing is going to happen, and that alone is also fact!

You must breath life into your dreams!

If you have faith, prove it, this may require from time to time some sweat equity. Put up or shut up - is another common phrase.

Do something that shows by your action, you're convinced and you believe and you will then by faith, receive!

Stay assertive, proactive, determined! Your mantra, however, can never be destructive, harmful or hurtful toward another, because that is not a mantra, that's a curse.

Your success, whether spiritual or physical, is never robbed from one and given away to benefit another.

We are a product of our belief system, good or bad, and we are always at the point where we are because of what our past actions have created.

No one else is credited, to blame, or responsible for where we are, only ourselves.

We are a product of our actions and our own personal belief system which proves the theory that our imagination coupled with our actions create our reality.

This, however, does not mean we are doomed, or for that matter guaranteed success. And unless we honor the truth, we are not truthful, and therefore, have no respect for what the truth is but possess only an empty desire to be something we don't deserve or understand.

To dishonor this reality puts us in a dangerous position where we could fall from grace with great and terrible destruction, destroying our credibility and all we have worked for in the process.

This is something more precious than riches. This luminous intelligible yet intangible possession must be guarded at every turn and especially from ourselves!

We have within each of us the ability to be diabolically self-destructive.

There is and has always been a living demon or spirit inside each of us, stalking us with temptation sometimes too strong to resist. Then on the other hand, throughout human history, there have been those born in extreme poverty, and because of their determination to rise from what others may see as impossible, have done so with such explosive results that they have changed the world for the better and everyone in it.

What are you made of?

Let me tell you. You are made of and for greatness. You possess the same genius and ability to do, go, and achieve whatever it is you feel strongly or passionate about.

The trigger that ignites your dream requires specific and undiluted action from you.

Your responsibility is to yourself, and it is within that responsibility that you'll become absorbed in an intense and focused determination to succeed.

You will do whatever it takes to keep the dream alive.

That will happen when you ultimately and clearly understand that your imagination is alive and lives within you for a reason.

No one else can give, create or hand over to you talent, passion, drive, or determination.

Passion and determination are part of all of our makeup, and is as important to us as any of our other vital organs that keep our body functioning while we are unconsciously sleeping or doing a multitude of other things.

Our subconscious functions independently of our conscious mind, and we hardly ever even pay much attention to it.

This must change, starting now, right where you are.

When you arrive at a clear understanding of who you are as a living, breathing entity, and understand the capacity you possess imaginatively then the possibilities are vividly all of a sudden alive and endless, instantaneous, and without restriction or limitation.

As we continue waking up to our ever unfolding imagination, it becomes obvious that nothing stands in our way that we don't allow or approve of.

By knowing this and acting on this truism, it becomes an astonishing breakthrough, and we feel like we have suddenly awakened from a deep sleep.

Suddenly and surprisingly, we start to realize we have been deprived, and the ones to blame for that crippling deprivation have fled. But let's not waste any time playing the blame game. Instead, let's get busy getting to know ourselves, our real selves, now that we finally have an invitation to this amazing opportunity.

Our strengths, our abilities, our passions now seem to be asking what we're going to do with our newfound freedom and awareness.

It is entirely up to us you know. Life is a gift, and gifts come to you from those who love you, treasure you, and have great expectation and admiration for you. Still a mystery?

Yes, but knowing so, puts the mystery under the all knowing all searching light and scrutiny of a different kind of revelation.

You've been handed something so powerful it suddenly seems confusing and unreal.

Remember this, with your newfound awareness of unlimited imagination, you cannot only move in any direction you choose or imagine without constraint, but you can operate and control every aspect of your reality.

What will you do or accomplish once you get to where you want to go? Or do you really have to go anywhere at all?

Remember this, the answer to any and everything will always remain within easy reach of our individual imaginations, if we will make a sincere effort to discover this spiritual power we possess.

There is nothing faster than your imagination, no device has ever been designed or conceived which can travel faster and farther than your imagination.

So far, nothing has been devised to measure or track the speed of thought, because that would differ in everyone.

You can travel faster and farther in a fraction of an instant of thought, and yet in the same fraction of that instant, return in the same nano second you just left in.

No one will ever suspect you were gone, not even yourself, unless you have started monitoring your thoughts and noting your actions.

We, all of us, do this constantly and mostly without even recognizing we're doing it.

It happens all the time. You've seen people go into this state of mind or blank kind of stare while in conversation with you, and through split attention and glazed over eyes never miss a beat but continue conversing.

Still, deep in thought, their attention is now divided but fully and functionally moving with such speed it is impossible to calculate.

Medically, it's referred to as a mild seizure, but people who find themselves in these trance like states while fully conscious and in the presence of others still having conversations, have just experienced such and never even realized it. This is supernatural and yet, still a very human function happening in all of us at different times.

They slip into their divided experience possibly because of something you might have said that triggered a thought in them.

Still they continue hearing you, talking and understanding everything you say, but are temporarily mentally swept into an experience splitting their attention between you and something or someone else of equal importance, for just a nano second or more.

Now that you are aware of this and in control of such a mighty steed, it is certainly impressive. But you have also acquired a most awesome responsibility.

Remember, when much is given much is required. Consider the meaning.

You have almost everything you need now, and in knowing this, you also have a power that at all cost you must control.

I am putting in your hands something that has always been yours, only now, it's active and alive.

Don't believe that tomorrow you'll wake up and think that all of what has happened was some kind of a mental shell game.

No, this will remain with you forever and set you on a continuing journey of self-enlightenment and discovery in hopes that you will keep evolving and lighting that path in everything you attempt, while everyone you meet will have no problem recognizing there is something about you that is indescribable.

You will read and re-read this book many times, and each time you ingest its meaning, it will reveal more and grow beyond what a thousand lifetimes will ever be able to contain.

Like the gravity that holds you fixed on earth, your imagination, just as real, just as powerful, will always be present and active, ready to serve you at your command.

Within you, there have always been powers that bend and shape reality without the physical touch.

Within your imagination lives the power to turn the flow of riches of all forms in your direction.

Within your imagination lives the reality that can provide perfect health.

Within your imagination is provision and formula for perfect love and within your imagination is the ability that can lead you to the gates of a new Eden.

There is no stopping you now, because you have reached the point where you cannot tell me of anything you can't imagine.

The awareness that we exist is the first experience we accept as real in our lives.

Going forward, people are able to use their imagination as a tool that creates understanding in all things without confusion, fear, effort, or uncertainty.

I know I have awakened in you a reality that will not permit you to remain still or yet return to those past hours of darkness ever again.

You will, from this point, advance within your enlightened state, recognizing the direction you have taken as a bold and daring move when so many will never hear, see, or experience the exhilaration that comes with such discovery.

Even though, you will be moving at the speed of your imagination and in the direction of your goal, physical life will always be lived in the present. And, because of this reality, you can neither catch the future or live even for one moment in the past, other than in memory.

The past shapes your future and transforms the present within you which allows you the ability to accept or reject what you experience as a free moral agent. This requires extreme caution.

What you do or experience presently, however, your memory will eventually discard, because you will have no need to remain in or try to return to the past for anything.

Remember this, the past is a closed door that can never be opened again, while the future is multiple doors that continually and automatically open as you evolve, as you rise through your many levels of awareness to achieve ultimate enlightenment.

This will continue growing in you as you continue on a positive and productive path gaining the knowledge suitable for your expression.

Nothing in the past will ever be productive or do you any good by refusing to let it go.

The biggest problem for everyone with fear of the future or the unknown simply is they have not yet overcome or been able to explain or identify the evidence of fear.

Some will refer to fear as sensory instinct and of cautionary value. It is not tangible, but clearly and obviously readable by the senses.

It's a readable sensation stemming back to ancient times when humanity was instinctive more than logical or intellectual.

Fear is an instinctive sensation and can serve you well in the case of fight or flight and in sensing when dangers are present.

We humans still walk that razor thin line that divide these two realities in us all.

We are capable of reasoning and negotiating at tense times. We're also capable of instinctively assessing almost any situation.

False evidence, however, doesn't and can't exist until we give it permission to do so.

Therefore, fear, like the ego, is identified as non-existent and results in nothing other than tricking you into robbing yourself of your own energy.

You simply allow it to happen, you permit it.

Remember this, it is you, you, who will be in charge of both the constructive and destructive.

You are free from your past and no longer asleep in drowsy inconsistency, so don't fall back into deception, captured by the very fear you just escaped from.

Your direction is forward, in front of you, into the light of awareness, leaving forever the horrors and confusion of the past life you were trapped in.

Knowledge, power, and understanding will help you shape and bend reality, and in doing so allow you to serve even a greater need.

Nothing could be greater than to rescue, inspire, and liberate others from greed driven governments, health care scams and deceptive structured religion.

What could be of greater service to humanity than to awaken in the unenlightened, these realities that you are now aware of?

You are in possession of something so powerful that it effects everyone you come in contact with.

Knowing that all things are possible is evidence of immense power and confirms unlimited ability.

Read that again, read the above verse multiple times every day and especially at the beginning and end of your day.

It's time to recognize the importance of who you are and the power you hold via your unlimited imagination.

Nothing happens until you've acknowledged and confirmed your faith has direct connection with creation.

With simple ease you will able to defy the laws of physics.

Using your imagination without propulsion you are able to bring into physical existence that which has never before existed.

Look around you at all the manmade examples - cars, books, toys, music, magnificent building structures, airplanes, ships, the ability to communicate digitally around the world with translation devices

These were all someone's ideas before becoming a physical reality.

This is proof that what I'm conveying to you presently is factual and realistic.

With your imagination now fully awake and possibilities endless, you must appreciate the fact that there are millions of people worldwide who create something everyday in order to survive without giving a single thought to the fact that others are naturally living in a constant and supernatural creative state of reality.

Why? How can this be so?

Because survival requires it, and it therefore, simply becomes routine. The same way your subconscious doesn't see monetary value in items you value because the subconscious is not impressed with wealth, but is there to satisfy your command only.

The nature of your subconscious is gratified through the accomplishment in getting you what you want without any emotion attached.

What does that say to you?

Put yourself in that state of mind, survival or success, just is, for the enlightened.

Watch what happens.

Be prepared to embrace and understand that our humanity is naturally creative in order that we may survive.

Everything in our physical life takes place along lines of natural ability. And, through our experience we become one with our environment's limitations, the same as a shark in an aquarium which only grows according to its environmental limit of up to possibly ten inches, but in the ocean, a shark will grow up to ten or twenty feet.

The awareness of our limited environment and the awakening of our imagination is another story altogether.

It doesn't come automatically to us when we're born like breathing does, but, it is learned over time and requires concentration and development.

It takes training, it takes controlling one's mind from wandering, and when it does wander, the effort of bringing it back and keeping it on track is the first order of the day if you are to survive.

The bible says renew your mind daily. Sounds simple enough. However, upon this understanding, it clearly becomes ritualistic.

You can see also the dedication required in such development, whatever your desire can be yours by setting the wheels of cause and effect in motion.

Don't forget, we just finished reading in the above that all things are possible to those who believe.

So to prove to yourself that you do believe, you simply do something about those dreams and take the first step of the journey.

I will tell you, without faith, commitment, and action in whatever it is you want to do, is wasted time and effort.

You must want success and believe passionately that you are deserving or you will find a way to fail unconsciously.
You will start proving by your actions you don't want success.

Honest self evaluation and understanding the reasons behind your motivation need to be up front and clearly understood before you invest precious time and effort.

Don't let anyone convince you that your reasons are less than honorable if it's only money you're interested in making, or if your interests are in things that differ from theirs. Because sometimes people are so sensitive they won't move forward when they feel intimidated or uncomfortable by negative opinion or condemnation from friends or associates.

Hello peer pressure!

Success comes in many ways and is unique in each individual.

Shake loose the tethers that hold you bound by others' opinions or legitimacy.

You are unique and as different as whatever your imagination will support, and that is limitless.

Your strengths are alive and within your power to think or imagine without restraint or concern of another's opinion.

Remember, your independence is a must if you are to maintain control of your life.

This does not by any means suggest that you shouldn't be sociable or uninvolved in societal matters.

What you think attracts others of like mind, and therefore, generates and supports the theory of strength in numbers all flowing in the same direction with a common cause. Otherwise, you have conflict and mass confusion.

This is a divergence and will only result in chaos.

When you reach this understanding and are able to control your thoughts and emotions, you will never again be servant to anyone or anything through force, addiction, intimidation, or fear, ever!

You will never explain yourself to anyone or feel the need to offer excuses or apologies for your actions.

There are only two types of people, the master and the servant.

At this stage, if you've been paying attention, consider yourself the former.

If you don't feel like you're in charge at this point, finish reading the book and then instantly read it again, and this time take it slow and analyze why you feel the way you do.

Take notes.

It is important that you start with a clear understanding who you are and what you've become first.

Addicts would find this action-based philosophy instant success, if in fact they are honestly seeking control over their negative and addictive habits.

Part Three

3

You will find that in your newfound power of imagination, you have become a man or woman of mental superiority, armed with wisdom as your weapon of choice.

You are creator of your fate because you have realized fate is not luck. Fate is developed and exists and lives comfortably secure in the depths of a controlled imagination.

You are actually living in another dimension of intelligence from those who accept life as it is and reality to be what they have been taught as a child.

Failing to grasp what they can't see or feel leaves some therefore only existing under another's opinion or power of influence.

To have ability, and to not use it shows you have not yet rid yourself of the enemies fear, doubt, shyness, low self-esteem, inaction, and lack of confidence.

Never let the rules rule you. Conformity is what you have been taught, and it reeks with failure.

You were born with genius ability. But like most, your caregivers' lack of creative imagination, education, and limited thought, including the ability and curiosity to know the unknown, never found its way into your mind.

You were born a genius, but being an innocent and unaware child, your decisions were redirected by those who thought they knew what was best for you.

Being a child, you were taught what your caregivers were taught. Instead of encouraging you to be imaginative, creative and expressive, many of you were persuaded to believe that others knew what was best because that's what they were taught to believe also.

As a child you learned the opposite of what you would have learned in the care of free, creative, forward thinkers.

Instinct and curiosity were your first original and natural gifts.
That sixth sense of awareness, that gut feeling, as referred to by many, is all natural and alive. But like the majority, this was compromised in your innocence and unsuspecting youth.

Don't worry though, nothing is ever lost, only misplaced. Through the retraining of your thinking and the reawakening of your natural talents and spirit, you will find you have years of fascinating discoveries and excitement in your future.

Don't blame those of the past for what they never knew. Move forward. You will see life differently tomorrow.

Look at how valuable you've become through discovering yourself.

There are others who like yourself had no idea who they were, and like you, unfortunately were also misdirected.

Consider all the new and amazing possibilities that come with this line of study.

It's fascinating and revolutionary, yet totally under your control.

New awareness is everywhere.

The four simple words, that have had the greatest impact on humanity to date is, "Let there be light!" Not just physical light, but the enlightenment of humanity.

Enlightenment and new possibilities are fast unfolding, and to our amazement, are filling our lives with more beautiful discovery than can ever be described.

Endless new discovery now and mind boggling wealth and enrichment become a personal thing that only you define from here on out.

Only you decide what is enough.

Imagination is a fabulous thing. I still recall someone telling me that one of Walt Disney's grade school teacher's told him he would never amount to much in life because he had no imagination. Whew!

You see, it isn't what others think of you, it's what you know about yourself, what you believe is possible, what you know is fact - proof, undeniable evidence, that we are co-creators with a God unlimited. It's how you use what you have that makes the difference in everything you will ever pursue.

I wonder how much other genius has been lost or never allowed to develop because someone misspoke and crushed an innocent and fragile imagination.
If the possible be considered, then the impossible must also be, because nothing is impossible.

Enter Einstein. His theories were so far advanced, no one but he understood them.

Only when he proved them, did the rest of the world accept them.

Is this where you are with something in your life?

It's one thing to have advanced ideas and knowledge. It's another to be able to prove them.

The ability to figure out a system, whereby you alone comprehend all of it, as in the case of the film maker James Cameron who developed the film Avatar.

James Cameron had previously written the script to Avatar years before the technology for shooting the film was even available.

He also developed the technology required in order to shoot the film.

Don't be fearful or reluctant to step out of the drudge and everyday commonality when and if you have something of importance you want to develop, say, or do.

The world is waiting to hear from you. You just have to be bold enough to stand out as an individual in a crowd of non-believers.

Those who reject this herd mentality, intuitively know already more than the scant ordinary and have no time for what is yesterday's news, but are already out front constantly scanning the horizons for elevated ideas and talented minds.

The movers and the shakers in this world are those who, with white hot imagination and intense determination, are able to see success before a project ever begins.

Those are the 20/20 visionaries standing ready with hearts pounding in anticipation of the challenge, prepared and readied for the magical moment to begin.

Let nothing, let no one negatively influence or diminish your creative thoughts or make you lose grip and fail to realize for one instant your creative identity, your determination, your genius, your uniqueness.

These are the most powerful assets you have, and along with passion, commitment, and fortitude, you are born to accomplish anything you pursue.

I want to make a point here and mention something all of us are guilty of.

There are negative elements living in all of us - laziness, procrastination, and broken motivation, to mention a few.

This is a new day in the life of a new you.

From this day forward, when something unique enters your mind, grab it, log it, and date it.

Explain in detail your thought or idea.

Explain the type of day or night it was, who you were with, and where you were.

The reason for this is so that you will be able to recall, feel, return to or relive the same state of mind you were in.

When you are ready to continue, you will be prepared, focused, and able to pursue the idea by recalling the feelings you had, the emotions and the excitement you felt, that surge, the rush.

Were you having coffee, tea, wine? Was it cold, warm, morning, noon, springtime?

What was special about that day or night?

You're going to need to revisit, re-familiarize yourself, and recall every detail, retrace your steps entering the room or location.

This is information you'll need to recall if you ever going to leave an idea on the table and return to it later.

Become an exceptional and a most thorough detective recalling every detail of your unique experience .

You'll want to feel those same sensations as you're recreating and recalling that electrifying surge of inspiration and discovery.

This may be something you're not used to, but when you start to recall that moment, you'll want to be in the same state of mind as you were in at the moment of discovery, feeling the same feelings and reliving all of those vivid moments and sensations.

You'll get used to this as you grow in your awareness, and it will eventually become as natural and automatic as falling asleep.

When it clicks and you're fully responsive to those sensations of recall, there will be a calm around you, and you will know that you know.

You won't be in a rush going nowhere, but sure of every step you take, confident that your awareness of self is supported by strong foundational evidence based in solid reality.

Your presence will speak for itself, no need of external substance to calm the jitters.

Your awareness will be calm and confident, free of confused uncertainty.

We can all recall times when life was like a bad dream, and even though we had a sense of being in control, our dream state told us we were not.

In our dream state no matter what we did or how we dressed we never felt in control, in style, comfortable or confident.

Dreams, though life like, present themselves in a way that feels real enough, yet frustrating and confusing, uncertain something mysterious keeps commanding our attention.

No matter what we do in our dream state to control the frustration, we continue experiencing it.

The reality, however, is that gaining control is always just inches out of reach or beyond our ability.

Whatever it is, is something we all need to clearly understand, identify, and fix in our waking hours and in our everyday lives.

Something will always be wrong in your dream state, always confusing, unless you get your life right while in your conscious and awakened state.

These dream experiences will always leave you confused and questioning what your dreams really mean.

Life in our presently unawakened state of who we think we are is exactly like a dream where there is never anything with total clarity or meaning but gives only the appearance of or impression that there is.

It's the same as a mirror's reflection of you. A reflection is that illusive something you can never capture or truly communicate with.

Fate lives in the reality of a clear and focused imagination.

What you do about controlling your imagination determines your fate and outcome.

We simply must reawaken in ourselves the powerfully charged, confident, determined, focused person we believe in, and at all cost get off the side roads and back on the freeway.

We are beginning to get glimpses of an entirely new and different reality here.

A powerfully controlled imagination, standing ready to serve, keeps us in our designated lane and connects us with the result we are seeking.

This is a battle, however, and it's something we must constantly be aware of and strive to control, and ultimately with time, overcome.

Your deadliest and most ferocious enemy in attaining what you envision, what you desire, what you dream of, is distraction, distraction, distraction, period!

When your focus is constantly toward your desire and believing you already possess it, you will find that it will surely manifest in your life.

We all experience uncertainty, internal conflicts, and an out of control, blurred or restricted focus of the bigger picture. We're bombarded with flack, and everything we don't want seems to be there interrupting our progress. These are the mountains that we must remove. As you all can see, we have work to do.

Read this book again, and again. You will find that by doing so, puts you lightyears ahead of those that fail to take the same initiative. Lastly, never entertain negativity. This is a constant battle for most. Learn to recognize its presence and lock it out of your mind. Refuse to entertain the presence of negativity at all cost, because it is your deadliest enemy, your downfall, your end!

www.ingramcontent.com/pod-product-compliance
Lightning Source LLC
Chambersburg PA
CBHW060556100426
42742CB00013B/2577